BOSTON COMMON PRESS
Brookline, Massachusetts

1999

Boston Common Press
17 Station Street
Brookline, Massachusetts 02445

ISBN 0-936184-35-3
Library of Congress Cataloging-in-Publication Data
The Editors of *Cook's Illustrated*
    How to make pot pies and casseroles: An illustrated step-by-step guide to preparing chicken pot pie, macaroni and cheese, shepherd's pie, turkey tetrazzini, lasagne, jambalaya, hoppin' john, and other streamlined casseroles./The Editors of *Cook's Illustrated*
1st ed.

    Includes 38 recipes and 29 illustrations
    ISBN 0-936184-35-3 (hardback): $14.95
    I. Cooking. I. Title
1999

Manufactured in the United States of America

Distributed by Boston Common Press, 17 Station Street, Brookline, MA 02445.

Cover and text design: Amy Klee
Recipe development: Bridget Lancaster, Kay Rentschler, Anne Yamanaka, and Dawn Yanagihara
Series editor: Jack Bishop

HOW TO MAKE POT PIES AND CASSEROLES

An illustrated step-by-step guide to preparing chicken pot pie, macaroni and cheese, shepherd's pie, turkey tetrazzini, lasagne, jambalaya, hoppin' john, and other streamlined casseroles.

THE COOK'S ILLUSTRATED LIBRARY

Illustrations by John Burgoyne

CONTENTS

introduction

O VER THE YEARS, MY VERMONT NEIGHBORS have served me just about every sort of casserole one can imagine, from those using local game like woodchuck (a bit greasy), rabbit (sublime), and squirrel (like chicken thighs) to turkey tettrazini and Brunswick stew. Our village is fond of covered-dish suppers, held at the grange or the church, so I have had my share of pot pies, white bean casseroles, and macaroni and cheese. Although casseroles have a bad name in this age of fava beans and goat cheese, they are real treasures—all-in-one main courses that require only a salad to complete the meal. So what makes the difference between a dull, over-cooked container of diner food and a truly great dish?

I discovered one of the secrets in James Beard's *American Cookery*. In a turkey tettrazini recipe, he suggests using a high heat and a shallow casserole so that the food cooks quickly, preserving fresh tastes and textures. We also found that the right preparation before the final baking is crucial. For example, green peas for a chicken pot pie can be added frozen, since they will cook with the other ingredients. Sauces should be thin, not thick and starchy. Balance between ingredients is critical—adding acidity to a chicken and rice casserole by using canned tomatoes perks up the flavors. Other techniques are simply an amalgam of common sense and good cooking. We hope this modest book puts casseroles and pot pies back into your repertoire of good food.

We have also published *How to Make a Pie, How to Make an American Layer Cake, How to Stir-Fry, How to Make Ice Cream, How to Make Pizza, How to Make Holiday Desserts, How to Make Pasta Sauces, How to Make Salad, How to Grill, How to Make Simple Fruit Desserts, How to Make Cookie Jar Favorites, How to Cook Holiday Roasts and Birds, How to Make Stew, How to Cook Shrimp and Other Shellfish, How to Barbecue and Roast on the Grill,* and *How to Cook Garden Vegetables.* Many other titles in this series will soon be available. To order other books, call us at (800) 611-0759 or visit our online bookstore at www.cooksillustrated.com. We are also the editors and publishers of *Cook's Illustrated,* a bimonthly publication about American home cooking. For a free trial copy of *Cook's,* call (800) 526-8442.

Christopher P. Kimball
Publisher and Editor
Cook's Illustrated

chapter one

CASSEROLE BASICS

THE CHALLENGE WHEN MAKING A GOOD casserole is keeping the ingredients as fresh tasting as possible. Too many casseroles are overcooked and dull, reminiscent of the worst cafeteria cuisine. That's because the ingredients are generally double-cooked. For example, pasta is boiled then baked and pot pie filling is stewed then baked. Our solution to all this cooking is to keep oven time to a minimum.

We found the best casseroles are made in a fairly shallow baking dish and cooked at a high oven temperature. This reduces cooking time to just a fraction of the time suggested in many cookbooks. Some casseroles can be in and out of the oven in just 15 minutes. Tasted against longer baking and slower ovens, this quick method wins hands down every time. Vegetables are fresher tasting (and looking), and pasta, grains, and beans have a better texture and are far less likely to be mushy.

The casserole comes in hundreds of different shapes and sizes. For the purposes of this book, we have limited ourselves to main-course casseroles.

We have divided the book into chapters based on the starch that holds the casserole together—pastry and biscuits (for pot pies), pasta, rice and grains, beans, and potatoes. Throughout, we have stayed true to the American spirit of these dishes, while using fresh ingredients of the highest quality. Yes, you can make a casserole with canned soup, but it won't taste as good as a casserole made with homemade sauce and vegetables you cook yourself. We think good results always justify an extra 10 minutes of work.

Our preference for fresh ingredients has, however, been coupled with an attempt to keep prep times as short as possible. Casseroles are meant to be convenience foods—a complete supper in a covered dish. There's no sense taking simple food and making it so complicated you would never make the recipe. We have consistently searched for shortcuts (like no-boil lasagne noodles and chicken pot pies that start with boneless, skinless breasts and canned broth) that deliver the best combination of flavor and convenience.

chapter two

POT PIES

W E WANTED TO FIGURE OUT A WAY TO streamline the process of making a pot pie. While it will never be a 20-minute meal, pot pie should not take all day to prepare. We started our testing with chicken pot pie and then decided to see if our experiences in the kitchen could be adapted to turkey and vegetable pot pies.

We began by determining the best way to cook the chicken. We steamed and roasted whole chickens, and we braised chicken parts. Steaming the chicken was time-consuming, requiring about one hour, and after that time the steaming liquid still didn't have enough flavor to make a

1 0

sauce for the pie. Roast chicken also required an hour in the oven, and by the time we took off the skin and mixed the meat in with the sauce and vegetables, the roasted flavor was lost. We had similar results with braised chicken: it lost its delicious flavor once the browned skin was removed.

Next we tried poaching, the most traditional cooking method. We tested this method both with bone-in parts and boneless, skinless breasts. Though both the parts and the breasts were poached in canned broth, we thought the long-simmered poaching liquid of the parts would be significantly better. But in our comparison of the pies, we found no difference in quality, and we were able to shave one-half hour off the cooking time (10 minutes to cook the breasts compared with 40 minutes to cook the parts). For those who like either dark or a mix of dark and white meat in the pie, boneless, skinless chicken thighs can be used as well.

We decided to tackle the vegetables next, so we made pies with raw vegetables, sautéed vegetables, and parboiled vegetables. We found that the vegetables sautéed before baking held their color and flavor best, the parboiled ones less so. The raw vegetables were not fully cooked at the end of baking time and gave off too much liquid, watering down the flavor and thickness of the sauce.

Our final task was to develop a sauce that was flavorful, creamy, and of the proper consistency. Chicken pot pie sauce is traditionally based on a roux (a mixture of butter and flour sautéed together briefly), which is thinned with chicken broth and often enriched with cream.

Because of the dish's inherent richness, we wanted to see how little cream we could get away with using. We tried three different pot pie fillings, with one-quarter cup of cream, one-quarter cup of half-and-half, and one cup of milk, respectively. Going into the oven, all the fillings seemed to have the right consistency and creaminess; when they came out, however, it was a different story. Vegetable and meat juices diluted the consistency and creaminess of the cream and half-and-half sauces. To achieve a creamy-looking sauce, we would have needed to increase the cream dramatically. Fortunately, we didn't have to try it, because we actually liked the milk-enriched sauce. The larger quantity of milk kept the sauce creamy in both color and flavor.

To keep the sauce from becoming too liquid, we simply added more flour. A sauce that looks a little thick before baking will become the perfect consistency after taking on the chicken and vegetable juices that release during baking.

As we expected, turkey pot pie followed the same rules as chicken pot pie. We found it most convenient to use left-over turkey meat, although if you can find turkey breast tenderloins in your supermarket, they may be prepared in the same way as boneless chicken breasts. As for vegetable pot pie, we found that a chicken pot pie minus the chicken tasted too light—it was more like a side dish than supper. To remedy this problem, we increased the amount of vegetables, especially hearty vegetables such as potatoes. Adding other root vegetables and dried mushrooms also helped to give vegetable pot pie enough heft.

Up until this point, we had been topping our pot pies with pastry dough. Although these crusts were delicious, we wondered if there were quicker, simpler options. Biscuits worked beautifully, although they were not much easier to prepare.

We tested phyllo pastry, which we thought would result in a light, flaky crust. To the contrary, we were surprised to find that the phyllo topping resulted in a tough, almost membrane-like cover. We then tried the frozen puff pastry found at most supermarkets. We were quite surprised at the lovely, puffed, light crust that appeared. After testing this pastry with a butter glaze, an egg wash glaze, and no glaze, we were happy to find that our tasters were unanimous in their preference for the plain pastry. The other advantage to using the puff pastry is the almost-perfect size of the sheets. They fit in a standard casserole dish without trimming.

♔

Master Recipe

Chicken Pot Pie

serves 6 to 8

➤ **NOTE:** *You can make the filling ahead of time, but remember to heat it on top of the stove before topping it. As for the topping, it can be made up to 2 hours in advance and refrigerated on a floured baking sheet. The pot pie can be baked in one large pan (a standard 13 x 9-inch pan is ideal, but feel free to use any baking dish with a similar surface area) or six individual ceramic baking dishes.*

1½	pounds boneless, skinless chicken breasts and/or thighs
2	cups chicken stock or canned low-sodium broth
1½	tablespoons vegetable oil
1	medium-large onion, finely chopped
3	medium carrots, peeled and cut crosswise ¼-inch thick
2	small celery stalks, cut crosswise ¼-inch thick
	Salt and ground black pepper

4		tablespoons unsalted butter
½		cup all-purpose flour
1½		cups milk
¼	~~½~~	teaspoon dried thyme
3		~~tablespoons dry sherry~~
2Tbls	~~¾~~	cup frozen green peas, thawed
3		tablespoons minced fresh parsley leaves
1		recipe Rich, Flaky Pie Dough (page 26), 1 recipe Fluffy Buttermilk Biscuits or variations (page 28), or 1 sheet (about 9 ounces) frozen puff pastry

▪▪ INSTRUCTIONS:

1. Adjust oven rack to low-center position; heat oven to 400 degrees. Put chicken and stock in small Dutch oven or soup kettle over medium heat. Cover, bring to a simmer; simmer until chicken is just done, 8 to 10 minutes. Transfer meat to large bowl, reserving broth in measuring cup for easy pouring later.

2. Increase heat to medium-high; heat oil in now-empty pan. Add onion, carrots, and celery; sauté until just tender, about 5 minutes. Season to taste with salt and pepper. While vegetables are sautéing, shred meat

15

into bite-sized pieces. Transfer cooked vegetables to bowl with chicken.

3. Heat butter over medium heat in same pan. When foaming subsides, add flour; cook about 1 minute, stirring. Whisk in chicken broth, milk, any accumulated chicken juices, and thyme. Bring to a simmer, then continue to simmer until sauce fully thickens, about 1 minute. Season to taste with salt and pepper; stir in sherry.

4. Pour sauce over chicken mixture; stir to combine. Stir in peas and parsley. Adjust seasonings. (The filling can be covered and refrigerated overnight; reheat before topping with pie dough, biscuits, or puff pastry.) Pour mixture into 13 x 9-inch pan or six 12-ounce ovenproof dishes. Top with pie dough (*see* figures 1 through 5, pages 18–20), biscuits (*see* figure 6, page 20), or puff pastry (*see* figures 7 and 8, page 21); bake until topping is golden brown and filling is bubbly, 30 minutes for a large pie and 20 to 25 minutes for individual pies. Serve hot.

⁙ **VARIATIONS:**

Chicken Pot Pie with Spring Vegetables

Herb Biscuits (page 29) are particularly good here.

Follow Master Recipe, replacing celery with 18 thin asparagus stalks that have been trimmed and cut into 1-inch pieces. Increase peas to 1 cup.

Chicken Pot Pie with Wild Mushrooms

The soaking liquid used to rehydrate dried porcini mushrooms replaces some of the chicken stock used to poach the chicken and then to enrich the sauce. This filling works well with Parmesan Biscuits (page 29).

Follow Master Recipe, soaking 1 ounce dried porcini mushrooms in 2 cups warm tap water until softened, about 20 minutes. Lift mushrooms from liquid, strain liquid, and reserve 1 cup. Use soaking liquid in place of 1 cup of chicken stock. Proceed with recipe, cooking rehydrated porcini and 12 ounces sliced button mushrooms with vegetables. Finish as directed.

Chicken Pot Pie with Corn and Bacon

This southern variation with corn and bacon works especially well with Cornmeal Biscuits (page 29).

Follow Master Recipe, replacing oil with ¼ pound bacon, cut crosswise into ½-inch-wide strips. Cook over medium heat until fat is rendered and bacon is crisp, about 6 minutes.

Remove bacon from pan with slotted spoon and drain on paper towels. Cook vegetables in bacon fat. Add drained bacon to bowl with chicken and cooked vegetables. Proceed with recipe, replacing peas with 2 cups fresh or frozen corn.

Turkey Pot Pie

Leftover turkey makes an excellent pot pie. If you want to use fresh turkey, replace chicken in Master Recipe with 1½ pounds turkey breast tenderloins. In step 1, increase simmering time to 9–11 minutes.

For leftover turkey, follow Master Recipe, replacing chicken with 3 cups cooked turkey meat, shredded into bite-sized pieces. Eliminate step 1 and use 2 cups chicken stock in step 3.

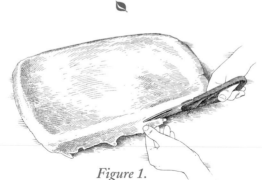

Figure 1.
If using pie dough, lay the rectangle of dough for the large pie or the dough rounds for the individual pies over the pot pie filling, trimming the dough to within ¾ inch of the pan lip.

Figure 2.
For a double-crust effect, simply tuck the overhanging dough down into the pan side. This tucked crust will become soft in the oven, like the bottom crust on a pie. Proceed to figure 5 if using this method.

Figure 3.
For a more finished look, tuck the overhanging dough back under itself so the folded edge is flush with the lip of the pan.

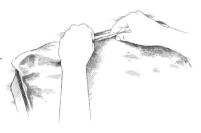

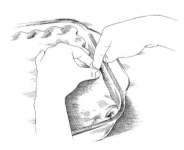

Figure 4.
Holding dough with thumb and index finger of one hand, push the dough with the index finger of the other hand to form a pleated edge. Repeat all around the edge to flute the dough.

19

Figure 5.
Cut at least four 1-inch vent holes in a large pot pie or one
1-inch vent hole in each individual pie.

Figure 6.
If using biscuits to top a pot pie, simply arrange the dough
rounds over the warm filling before baking.

Figure 7.

If using store-bought puff pastry, defrost the dough until pliable but still chilled, 20 to 30 minutes. Unfold and place with creases opening onto a floured surface like a book set face down.

Figure 8.

Roll the defrosted puff pastry out so that it is about two inches larger than the baking dish(es). Lay the puff pastry over the filling. Tuck the edges of the pastry into the pan (see figure 2) or flute the edges (see figures 3 and 4). Cut vent holes as in figure 5.

♛

Master Recipe

Vegetable Pot Pie
serves 6 to 8

➤ NOTE: *The abundant use of vegetables makes this pie hearty enough to serve as a main course. If you like, use chicken broth in place of the vegetable broth.*

3	tablespoons vegetable oil
1	medium-large onion, finely chopped
4	medium carrots, peeled and cut crosswise ¼-inch thick
2	small celery stalks, cut crosswise ¼-inch thick
2	medium garlic cloves, finely minced
5	medium red-skinned potatoes, cut into ½-inch dice
24	asparagus spears, trimmed and cut into 1-inch pieces
	Salt and ground black pepper
4	tablespoons unsalted butter
½	cup all-purpose flour
2	cups vegetable stock

1½   cups milk

½   teaspoon dried thyme

3   tablespoons dry sherry

¾   cup frozen green peas, thawed

3   tablespoons minced fresh parsley leaves

1   recipe Rich, Flaky Pie Dough (page 26),
1 recipe Fluffy Buttermilk Biscuits or
variations (page 28), or 1 sheet
(about 9 ounces) frozen puff pastry

■■ INSTRUCTIONS:

1. Heat oil in medium Dutch oven or soup kettle over medium-high heat. Add onion, carrots, and celery; sauté 3 minutes. Add garlic and potatoes, cover, and cook for 5 minutes, stirring occasionally. Add asparagus, cover again, and cook for 4 minutes, stirring occasionally. Season to taste with salt and pepper. Transfer cooked vegetables to bowl.

2. Heat butter over medium heat in empty pan. When foaming subsides, add flour; cook about 1 minute, stirring. Whisk in vegetable stock, milk, and thyme. Bring to a simmer, then continue to simmer until sauce fully thickens, about 1 minute. Season to taste with salt and pepper; stir in sherry.

3. Pour sauce over vegetable mixture; stir to combine. Stir in peas and parsley. Adjust seasonings. (The filling can be covered and refrigerated overnight; reheat before topping with pie dough, biscuits, or puff pastry.) Pour mixture into 13 x 9-inch pan or six 12-ounce ovenproof dishes. Top with pie dough (*see* figures 1 through 5, pages 18–20), biscuits (*see* figure 6, page 20), or puff pastry (*see* figures 7 and 8, page 21); bake until topping is golden brown and filling is bubbly, 30 minutes for a large pie and 20 to 25 minutes for individual pies. Serve hot.

VARIATIONS:

Vegetable Pot Pie with Winter Root Vegetables

Follow Master Recipe, decreasing potatoes to 4 medium and adding 3 medium parsnips, peeled and cut crosswise, ¼-inch thick, and 1 medium turnip, peeled and cut into ½-inch dice, with garlic and potatoes in step 1. Increase cooking time to 9 minutes. Omit asparagus. Season with salt and pepper to taste and proceed as directed.

Vegetable Pot Pie with Wild Mushrooms

The soaking liquid used to rehydrate dried porcini mushrooms replaces some of the vegetable stock used to enrich the sauce. Parmesan Biscuits (page 29) are particularly good in this recipe.

Follow Master Recipe, soaking 1 ounce dried porcini mushrooms in 2 cups warm tap water until softened, about 20 minutes. Lift mushrooms from liquid, chop mushrooms, strain liquid, and reserve, adding enough vegetable stock to make up 2 cups of liquid. Proceed with recipe, adding reserved porcini mushrooms along with 10 ounces sliced white button mushrooms, 4 ounces sliced shiitake mushrooms, and 8 ounces sliced cremini mushrooms along with garlic; cover the pot and cook for 6 minutes. Add potatoes, cover, and cook 5 minutes more. Omit asparagus. Season with salt and pepper to taste and proceed as directed.

Rich, Flaky Pie Dough

Makes enough dough to cover one 13 x 9-inch baking
dish or six 12-ounce ovenproof baking dishes

➤ **NOTE:** *We find that a combination of butter and shortening
delivers the best texture and flavor for pie pastry. Use a food
processor to cut the fat into the flour. Once the mixture resembles
coarse cornmeal, turn it into a bowl and add just enough ice water
to bring the dough together. If you like a bottom crust in your pot
pie, you can duplicate that soft crust texture by tucking any overhanging dough down into the pan side rather than fluting it.*

1½	cups all-purpose flour
½	teaspoon salt
8	tablespoons (1 stick) unsalted butter, chilled, cut into ¼-inch pieces
4	tablespoons chilled all-vegetable shortening
3 to 4	tablespoons ice-cold water

⁝ INSTRUCTIONS:

1. Mix flour and salt in workbowl of food processor fitted
with steel blade. Scatter butter pieces over flour mixture,
tossing to coat butter with flour. Cut butter into flour with
five 1-second pulses. Add shortening; continue pulsing
until flour is pale yellow and resembles coarse cornmeal,
keeping some butter bits size of small peas, about four more
1-second pulses. Turn mixture into medium bowl.

2. Sprinkle 3 tablespoons of ice-cold water over mixture. Using rubber spatula, fold water into flour mixture. Then press down on dough mixture with broad side of spatula until dough sticks together, adding up to 1 tablespoon more cold water if dough will not come together. Shape dough into ball, then flatten into 4-inch disk. Wrap dough in plastic and refrigerate for 30 minutes while preparing pie filling.

3. On floured surface, roll dough into 15 x 11-inch rectangle, about ⅛-inch thick. If making individual pies, roll dough ⅛-inch thick and cut 6 dough rounds about 1 inch larger than pan circumference.

4. Lay dough over the warm pot pie filling, trimming dough to within ¾ inch of pan lip. Tuck overhanging dough back under itself so folded edge is flush with lip of pan and flute edges all around. Or, simply tuck overhanging dough down into pan side. Cut at least four 1-inch vent holes in large pot pie or one 1-inch vent hole in smaller pies. (*See* figures 1–5, pages 18-20, for illustrations on preparing crust for baking.) Proceed with pot pie recipe.

Fluffy Buttermilk Biscuits

Makes enough to cover one 13 x 9-inch baking dish or six 12-ounce ovenproof baking dishes

➤ **NOTE:** *When making fluffy buttermilk biscuits, we use the food processor to cut the butter into the dry ingredients. We then scrape this mixture into a bowl and stir in the buttermilk. If you like, substitute an 8-ounce container of low-fat or whole-milk plain yogurt for the buttermilk. If the dough does not quite come together, add 1 or 2 tablespoons regular milk. Do not overwork the biscuits. Unlike pie pastry, biscuits take to a number of different flavorings.*

1	cup all-purpose flour
1	cup cake flour (not self-rising)
2	teaspoons baking powder
¼	teaspoon baking soda
¼ ~~1~~	teaspoon sugar
½	teaspoon salt
8	tablespoons (1 stick) unsalted butter, chilled and quartered lengthwise and cut crosswise into ¼-inch pieces
¾	cup cold buttermilk, plus 1 to 2 tablespoons extra, if needed

⦂ INSTRUCTIONS:

1. Pulse first six ingredients in workbowl of food processor fitted with steel blade. Add butter; pulse until mixture resembles coarse meal with a few slightly larger butter lumps.

2. Transfer mixture into medium bowl; add ¾ cup buttermilk; stir with fork until dough gathers into moist clumps. Add remaining 1 or 2 tablespoons buttermilk if dough is too dry. Transfer dough to floured work surface and form into rough ball, then roll dough ½-inch thick. Using 2½- to 3-inch pastry cutter, stamp out 8 rounds of dough. If making individual pies, cut dough slightly smaller than circumference of each dish.

3. Arrange dough rounds over warm filling (*see* figure 6, page 20) and proceed with pot pie recipe.

∷ VARIATIONS:

Parmesan Biscuits

Follow recipe for Fluffy Buttermilk Biscuits, decreasing the butter to 5 tablespoons. After fat has been processed into flour and transferred to medium bowl, add 1½ cups grated Parmesan cheese (4 ounces); toss lightly, then stir in liquid.

Herb Biscuits

Follow recipe for Fluffy Buttermilk Biscuits, adding 3 tablespoons minced parsley or 2 tablespoons minced fresh parsley leaves and 1 tablespoon minced fresh tarragon or dill leaves after fat has been processed into flour.

Cornmeal Biscuits

Follow recipe for Fluffy Buttermilk Biscuits, replacing cake flour with 1 cup yellow cornmeal.

chapter three

❧

PASTA CASSEROLES

THIS CHAPTER EXPLORES SEVERAL AMERI-can and Italian casseroles that start with pasta: turkey tetrazzini, macaroni and cheese, baked ziti, and lasagne.

Turkey tetrazzini can be very good, an interesting blend of toasted bread crumbs, silky sauce, and turkey meat, bound together by one of our favorite foods, spaghetti. Or, it can taste like cafeteria food. The downside of casseroles—that individual tastes and textures are fused and thus diminished—is acute with this dish. We found that baking the casserole in a shallow dish in a hot oven to prevent overcooking makes a big difference in this recipe.

Next we adjusted the sauce. The traditional choice is béchamel, a sauce in which milk is added to a roux, a whisked mixture of melted butter and flour. We decided to use a velouté, a sauce based on chicken stock. This brightened up both the texture and the flavor, since dairy tends to dampen other flavors. We also played around a bit with the amount of sauce, trying larger and smaller quantities, and found that more sauce overran the taste of the other ingredients. In this case, less was more. The dish still needed a burst of flavor, however, so we spruced it up with a shot of sherry and a little lemon juice and nutmeg, a bit of Parmesan cheese to provide tang and bite, and a full two teaspoons of fresh thyme.

Most recipes do not toast the bread crumbs before baking. This step does complicate the dish by adding an extra step (in a pinch, you can skip the toasting), but it is well worth it. Tossing the toasted bread crumbs with a bit of grated Parmesan also helps to boost their flavor.

Macaroni and cheese is another classic American pasta casserole. There are two distinct styles of macaroni and cheese. The more common variety is béchamel-based. Here macaroni is blanketed with a cheese-flavored white sauce, usually topped with crumbs, and baked. The other variety is custard-based. In this style, a mixture of egg and milk is poured over layers of grated cheese and noodles. As the dish bakes, the eggs, milk, and cheese set into a custard. This macaroni and cheese is also topped with bread crumbs.

We tried both styles and were unimpressed. The béchamel-based version was grainy and tasted like macaroni with cheese sauce. We preferred the cheesier-flavored custard version, but this dish still had problems—the dry custard had set around the noodles. Neither recipe had done the job of melding the cheese sauce and macaroni.

We then ran across a recipe in John Thorne's *Simple Cooking* (Penguin, 1989). His recipe starts with macaroni cooked just shy of al dente. The hot, drained macaroni is then tossed with butter in a heatproof pan or bowl. Evaporated milk, hot red pepper sauce, dry mustard, eggs, and a large quantity of cheese are stirred into the noodles. The combination is baked for 20 minutes, with cheese and milk additions and a thorough stir every 5 minutes. Frequent stirrings allow the eggs to thicken without setting, which results in an incredibly silky sauce. During cooking, the sauce settles into the tubular openings of the macaroni, offering a burst of cheese with each new bite. The results were fantastic.

Though the recipe was virtually perfect, we did consider a few refinements. First, we found that at the end of baking, the dish was hot but hardly piping. We also missed the contrasting textures of crunchy bread crumbs and soft noodles and sauce offered by the baked versions. Finally, we wondered if evaporated milk was really necessary.

After testing the recipe with whole and low-fat milks and half-and-half, we realized that evaporated milk was not an ingredient thoughtlessly added. All the macaroni and cheese dishes made with fresh milk curdled a bit, resulting in a chalky, grainy texture. The one made with evaporated milk remained silky smooth. The evaporation and sterilization process stabilizes the milk, which in turn stabilizes the macaroni and cheese.

We found that you could not remedy the dish's luke-warm temperature problem by leaving it in the oven much longer than the suggested 20 minutes. If you do, you run the risk of curdling the eggs, and the dish starts to develop a subtle grainy texture. We wondered if we could cook the macaroni and cheese on top of the stove instead of in the oven. We found that by using a heavy-bottomed pot and cooking over low heat, it was possible to make the macaroni and cheese on top of the stove in less than five minutes. Not only was this method quicker, but it kept the macaroni and cheese piping hot. To add the standard bread crumb topping, we poured the macaroni and cheese in a casserole dish, sprinkled on the bread crumbs, and ran the dish under the broiler for several minutes.

With our classic American pasta casseroles perfected, we

turned to baked ziti. This dish, with tomato sauce and mozzarella cheese, can be a delicious Italian casserole, or it can be dry and unappetizing, with hard, overcooked noodles. The key to avoiding these problems is to keep the pasta in the oven as briefly as possible and to use enough tomato sauce. When we just coated the noodles lightly with sauce, they tended to become dry and hard in the oven. Adding a little cooking water to the drained pasta also helped keep the casserole moist.

Aside from the pasta and tomato sauce, cheese is the other major component of this dish. If you can, use fresh mozzarella packed in water, which makes the texture of the finished dish especially moist and creamy. Mozzarella is a bit bland. We found that adding a quarter cup of Parmesan perks up the flavor. To ensure that the cheese is evenly distributed throughout the casserole, layer half of the pasta in the baking dish, sprinkle with half of the cheeses, then add the remaining pasta and cheeses and, finally, the sauce.

Lasagne made with no-boil noodles is another good example of a quick, satisfying casserole. These precooked, dried noodles eliminate the time-consuming step of boiling and draining the sheets of pasta; the noodles may simply be layered straight from the box into a baking dish with tomato sauce and cheese.

The challenge in creating this recipe was to figure out

how to use the no-boil noodles. We tried them in a standard lasagne and found that they sucked all the moisture out of the sauce, leaving tiny bits of dried-out tomato pulp. The noodles were stiff, even crunchy in places. Clearly, the noodles needed more moisture to rehydrate.

The label on one brand of noodles suggested adding stock to the assembled lasagne. The result was a watery mess. We tried another manufacturer's suggestion to soak the noodles in hot water before layering them into the pan. This, too, caused the noodles to cook up soft and mushy.

We made some headway when we covered the pan with foil before it went into the oven. The steam trapped by the foil helped the noodles to soften without causing the sauce to dry out. Using more tomato sauce than you might in a standard lasagne with boiled noodles also helped rehydrate the noodles. We found that leaving the tomato sauce fairly watery (we simmered it for just five minutes) and then adding some water provided enough moisture, helping to make the pasta tender without becoming too soft.

Covering the lasagne with foil as it bakes does present one problem-the top layer of cheese won't brown. This was easily solved be removing the foil during the last 15 minutes of baking.

Turkey Tetrazzini

serves 6

➤ **NOTE:** *Using a shallow baking dish, no cover, and a very hot oven benefit both texture and flavor. Don't be stingy with the salt and pepper. Tetrazzini is great with leftover chicken as well.*

Topping

1	cup fresh bread crumbs (*see* figures 9 through 11, pages 38–39)
	Pinch salt
1½	tablespoons unsalted butter, melted
¼	cup grated Parmesan cheese

Filling

	Salt
¾	pound spaghetti or other long-strand pasta
6	tablespoons butter, plus extra for greasing baking dish
8	ounces white button mushrooms, wiped clean, stems trimmed, and sliced thin
2	medium onions, minced
	Ground black pepper
¼	cup all-purpose flour
2	cups chicken stock or canned low-sodium chicken broth
3	tablespoons dry sherry

36

¾   cup grated Parmesan cheese

¼   teaspoon grated nutmeg

2   teaspoons fresh lemon juice

2   teaspoons minced fresh thyme leaves

4   cups leftover cooked boneless turkey or chicken meat, cut into ¼-inch dice

2   cups frozen peas, thawed

INSTRUCTIONS:

1. *For the topping:* Adjust oven rack to middle position and heat oven to 350 degrees. Mix bread crumbs, salt, and butter in small baking dish; bake until golden brown and crisp, 15 to 20 minutes. Cool to room temperature, transfer to bowl, and mix with ¼ cup grated Parmesan.

2. *For the filling:* Increase oven temperature to 450 degrees. Butter shallow casserole or baking dish that measures about 13 x 9 inches. Bring 4 quarts water to boil in large pot. Add 1 tablespoon salt, snap spaghetti in half, and add to pot. Cook until al dente. Reserve ¼ cup of cooking water, drain spaghetti, and return to pot with reserved liquid.

3. Meanwhile, heat 2 tablespoons butter in large skillet over medium heat until foaming subsides; add mushrooms and onions and sauté, stirring frequently, until onions soften and mushroom liquid evaporates, 7 to 10 minutes. Season to taste with salt and pepper; transfer to medium bowl and set aside.

4. Melt remaining 4 tablespoons butter in cleaned skillet over medium heat. When foam subsides, whisk in flour and cook, whisking constantly, until flour turns golden, 1 to 2 minutes. While continuing to whisk, gradually add chicken stock. Adjust heat to medium-high and simmer until mixture thickens, 3 to 4 minutes. Off heat and whisk in sherry, Parmesan, nutmeg, ½ teaspoon salt, lemon juice, and thyme. Add sauce, mushroom mixture, turkey, and peas to spaghetti and mix well, adjusting seasonings to taste.

5. Turn mixture into buttered baking dish, sprinkle evenly with bread crumbs, and bake until bread crumbs brown and mixture is bubbly, 13 to 15 minutes. Serve immediately.

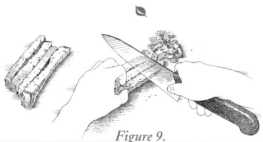

Figure 9.

Fresh crumbs are worth the minimal effort they require. We find that dry bread crumbs are powdery and tasteless. Fresh bread crumbs may be cut with a knife, grater, or food processor. To make bread crumbs by hand, use a sharp bread knife to cut slices ⅜-inch thick. Cut these slices into ⅜-inch strips, then cut these into cubes and chop the crumbs until they are about the size of dried black beans.

Figure 10.
To make bread crumbs with a box grater, rub the trimmed bread
against the largest holes. The crumbs will be finer-textured than
those made by hand or in a food processor.

Figure 11.
To make bread crumbs in a food processor, cut the trimmed loaf
into 1½-inch cubes, then pulse the cubes in a food processor
to the desired crumb size.

"Baked" Macaroni and Cheese
serves 4 as a main course or 6 to 8 as a side dish

➤ **NOTE:** *Our preferred version of macaroni and cheese turned out to be a simple stove-top recipe that cooks in five minutes. To finish the dish, we sprinkle it with fresh bread crumbs and put it under the broiler for a minute or two, which gives it that baked casserole look with a golden-brown topping.*

6	tablespoons unsalted butter
1	cup fresh bread crumbs (*see* figures 9 through 11, pages 38–39)
	Salt
12	ounces sharp Wisconsin cheddar, American, or Monterey Jack cheese, shredded (about 3 cups)
2	large eggs
1	can (12 ounces) evaporated milk
¼	teaspoon hot red pepper sauce
1	teaspoon dry mustard, dissolved in 1 teaspoon water
12	ounces elbow macaroni
	Ground black pepper

⁞ INSTRUCTIONS:

1. Heat 2 tablespoons butter in large skillet over medium heat until foam subsides. Add bread crumbs and cook, tossing to coat with butter, until crumbs just begin to color.

Season to taste with salt. Cool completely, toss with ¼ cup cheese, and set aside.

2. Adjust oven rack 6 inches from heating element and heat broiler.

3. Mix eggs, 1 cup evaporated milk, pepper sauce, and mustard mixture in small bowl and set aside.

4. Meanwhile, bring 3 quarts water to boil in large pot. Add 2 teaspoons salt and macaroni and cook until almost tender but still a little firm to the bite. Drain and return pasta to pot over low heat. Add remaining 4 tablespoons butter and toss to melt.

5. Pour egg mixture over buttered noodles along with three-quarters of remaining cheese. Stir until thoroughly combined and cheese starts to melt. Gradually add remaining milk and cheese, stirring constantly, until mixture is hot and creamy, about 5 minutes. Season with salt and pepper to taste.

6. Pour cooked macaroni and cheese into 9-inch square baking dish. Spread crumbs evenly over top. Broil until crumbs turn deep brown, 1 to 2 minutes. Let stand to set a bit, about 5 minutes, and serve.

Master Recipe

Baked Ziti with Mozzarella and Tomatoes

serves 6

➤ **NOTE:** *Use fresh mozzarella if possible—it will provide extra creaminess and moisture, which are important in this dish.*

2	tablespoons extra-virgin olive oil, plus more for oiling baking dish
2	medium garlic cloves, minced
1	can (28 ounces) crushed tomatoes
2	tablespoons coarsely chopped fresh basil leaves
	Salt
1	pound ziti or other short, tubular pasta
8	ounces mozzarella cheese, shredded
½	cup grated Parmesan cheese

∷ INSTRUCTIONS:

1. Preheat oven to 400 degrees. Heat 2 tablespoons oil and garlic in a medium skillet over medium heat until fragrant but not brown, about 2 minutes. Stir in tomatoes; simmer until thickened slightly, about 10 minutes. Stir in basil and salt to taste.

2. Meanwhile, bring 4 quarts water to boil in large pot. Add 1 tablespoon salt and pasta. Cook until almost tender but still a little firm to the bite. Reserve ¼ cup of cooking water, drain pasta, and return it to pot with reserved liquid. Stir in tomato sauce.

3. Lightly brush 13 x 9-inch baking dish with oil. Pour half of pasta into dish. Sprinkle with half of mozzarella and half of Parmesan. Pour remaining pasta into dish and sprinkle with remaining mozzarella and Parmesan.

4. Bake until cheese turns golden brown, about 20 minutes. Remove dish from oven and let rest for 5 minutes before serving.

▋▋ V A R I A T I O N S :

Baked Ziti with Eggplant

Cut 2 medium eggplants (about 2 pounds) crosswise into
¾-inch-thick slices, then into ¾-inch-thick strips. Place
eggplant in colander and sprinkle with 1 tablespoon kosher
salt. Set over bowl for 1½ hours. Brush off salt. Heat 3
tablespoons oil in large skillet. Add eggplant and cook over
medium-low heat until eggplant is tender, 15 to 20 minutes. Add garlic to pan (eliminate the 2 tablespoons oil) and
proceed with recipe as directed.

Baked Ziti with Meatballs

Follow Master Recipe, adding 1 recipe cooked and drained
Best Meatballs to cooked tomato sauce. Proceed as directed.

Best Meatballs
makes several dozen tiny meatballs

2	slices white sandwich bread torn into small cubes (crust discarded)
½	cup buttermilk or 6 tablespoons plain yogurt thinned with 2 tablespoons whole milk
¾	pound ground chuck mixed with ¼ pound ground pork, or 1 pound ground chuck
¼	cup grated Parmesan cheese
2	tablespoons minced fresh parsley leaves
1	large egg yolk
1	small garlic clove, minced
¾	teaspoon salt
	Ground black pepper
	Vegetable oil

▋▋ INSTRUCTIONS:

1. Combine bread and buttermilk in small bowl, mashing occasionally until smooth paste forms, about 10 minutes.

2. Combine bread mixture, meat, cheese, parsley, egg yolk, garlic, salt, and pepper to taste in a medium bowl until well blended.

3. Heat about ¼ inch of vegetable oil in large skillet. Take a

45

handful of meat mixture and, working directly over skillet, pinch off pieces no larger than a small grape, then flatten them slightly (*see* figure 12). Cooking in batches to avoid overcrowding, carefully drop them into hot oil. Fry, turning once, until evenly browned, 3 to 4 minutes. Use a slotted spoon to transfer meatballs to a paper towel on platter.

Figure 12.

Casseroles require small meatballs that won't overwhelm the other ingredients. Rather than shaping lots of round little meatballs, simply pinch off small pieces of the meatball mixture right over the skillet. Each piece should be no larger than a small grape.

♛

Master Recipe

Quick Lasagne with Meatballs
serves 6 to 8

➤ NOTE: *Make sure to buy American no-boil noodles, which are long and thin. In our testing, we found that square Italian no-boil noodles taste great, but their odd shape makes them difficult to use in a standard casserole dish.*

2	tablespoons olive oil
2	medium garlic cloves, minced
1	can (28 ounces) crushed tomatoes
2	tablespoons chopped fresh basil or parsley leaves
	Salt and ground black pepper
15	dried 7 x 3½-inch no-boil lasagne noodles
1	recipe Best Meatballs (pages 45–46)
1	pound mozzarella cheese, shredded (about 4 cups)
⅔	cup grated Parmesan cheese

47

♛

Master Recipe
Quick Lasagne with Meatballs

▓ INSTRUCTIONS:

1. Heat oil and garlic in medium skillet over medium heat until fragrant but not brown, about 2 minutes. Stir in tomatoes; simmer until thickened slightly, about 10 minutes. Stir in basil or parsley and salt and pepper to taste. Pour into large measuring cup. Add enough water to make 3½ cups.

2. Spread ½ cup sauce evenly over bottom of greased 13 x 9-inch baking dish. Lay three noodles crosswise over sauce, making sure they do not touch each other or sides of the pan. Spread ¼ of prepared meatballs evenly over noodles, ½ cup sauce evenly over meatballs, and ¾ cup mozzarella and 2 tablespoons Parmesan evenly over sauce. Repeat layering of noodles, meatballs, sauce, and cheeses three more times. For fifth and final layer, lay final three noodles crosswise over previous layer and top with remaining 1 cup tomato sauce, 1 cup mozzarella, and 2 generous tablespoons Parmesan. (Can be wrapped with plastic and refrigerated overnight or wrapped in plastic and aluminum foil and frozen for up to 1 month. If frozen, defrost in refrigerator.)

3. Adjust oven rack to middle position and heat oven to 375 degrees. Cover pan with large sheet foil greased with cooking spray. Bake 25 minutes (30 minutes if chilled); remove foil and continue baking until top turns golden brown in spots, about 15 minutes. Remove pan from oven and let lasagne rest 5 minutes. Cut and serve immediately.

▪▪ VARIATION:

Quick Lasagne with Roasted Zucchini and Eggplant

Adjust oven racks to upper- and lower-middle positions and heat oven to 400 degrees. Toss 1 pound each zucchini (about 2 medium) and eggplant (about 2 small), cut into ½-inch dice, with 3 tablespoons extra-virgin olive oil, 4 minced garlic cloves, and salt and pepper to taste. Spread out vegetables on two greased baking sheets; roast, turning occasionally, until golden brown, about 35 minutes. Set vegetables aside. Proceed with Master Recipe, replacing meatballs with roasted zucchini and eggplant.

chapter four

RICE & GRAIN CASSEROLES

GRAINS ARE EXCELLENT CANDIDATES FOR casseroles for several reasons. Hearty and filling yet also fairly bland, they work well as a background for many, many flavors.

Rice is the most obvious choice for a grain casserole because it is so familiar to American cooks. We wanted to develop a recipe for chicken and rice casserole and then see if we could adapt this recipe to make the Creole specialty known as jambalaya, with its rice, sausage, and shrimp.

There are two recurring problems with most chicken and rice casseroles. The rice tends to cook unevenly, becoming hard and brittle in some spots and soggy and mushy in others. The other issue is the cooking of the chicken. The breast meat tends to dry out and overcook by the time the legs and thighs are done.

We decided to tackle the chicken issue first. The parts are first sautéed to build flavor and then placed in a baking dish with the rice and other seasonings. We solved the problem of overcooked breast meat by adding the browned legs and thighs to the baking dish at the outset. We reserved the browned breast pieces and added them to the casserole halfway through its cooking time.

At this point in our testing we decided to jettison the chicken wings from our recipe. The wings are covered with a lot of thick skin that does not take well to "casseroling." Chicken wings are best grilled, so excess fat can be rendered and the skin can turn crisp. What's more, when we served the wings from the casserole they looked pretty paltry on the plate; they just didn't make up a complete serving, as did the other parts of the chicken.

With the chicken issues resolved, we turned our attention to the rice. In our first attempts, the rice on top of the baking dish became brittle and dry and the rice at the bottom of the dish was a bit soggy. We found that stirring the rice once solved this problem. To stir the rice easily, we found it best to transfer the chicken thighs and legs to a plate and then stir up the rice. The chicken thighs and legs can be placed back on top of the rice along with the browned breast pieces.

We tested various liquids used to cook the rice in the casseroles. Chicken stock made a very heavy dish, while plain water was bland. Adding some wine and canned tomatoes to plain water proved to be the right balance. The acidity in the wine and tomatoes enriched the flavor of the chicken and rice without adding heaviness.

As for the choice of rice, we found that regular long-grain rice works well. Parboiled (or converted) rice was tasteless by comparison. Medium-grain rice made a creamier casserole, more like risotto, which some tasters liked and others didn't. Basmati rice cooked up fluffy and nutty and seemed to make the most sense with the Indian spice variation.

We found that jambalaya, the famed Creole rice casserole, can be made along the same lines as a chicken and rice casserole. Jambalaya contains sausage, which can be treated just like chicken—browned, removed from the pan, and then added to the baking dish with the rice and liquid. Shrimp is a bit trickier since it cooks so quickly. We found it best not to precook the shrimp but to add raw shrimp when the casserole is almost done.

We found that pearl barley, just like rice, can be used to make casseroles. Barley becomes starchier and creamier when cooked this way. Sweet Italian sausage works well with the earthy flavors of the barley. Mushrooms are another obvious addition to a barley casserole.

The last recipe in this chapter is a polenta pie, a particularly rich Italian casserole. This dish relies on cooked cornmeal mush (called polenta) to bind together a filling, which is usually tomato based. A polenta pie is akin to a lasagne (the polenta takes the place of pasta) or even a pot pie (the polenta acts like a crust). We tested various kinds of polenta pie and ended up liking those with a bottom and top crust best.

To prevent lumps from forming, we found it best to stir the cornmeal into room-temperature liquid and then add this liquid directly to simmering water. Polenta made with all water was a bit bland. Adding some chicken broth improved the flavor. We found that using all broth, however, was a mistake. It tended to make the polenta compete with, rather than complement, the filling. A ratio of four parts water to one part stock proved to be ideal.

We also found that the polenta mixture quickly became stiff and hard to work with. Adding some butter as the polenta cooks helps keep it slightly loose and improves the flavor of the polenta layers. If it still solidifies (this might happen if you take a break when assembling the casserole), you can loosen the texture by stirring in some hot water.

⩚

Master Recipe

Chicken and Rice Casserole

serves 6

➤ **NOTE:** *We prefer not to use chicken wings in casseroles. They are mostly flabby skin with very little meat and make a poor serving, especially when compared with the breast, leg, or thigh. If you are trying to stretch a casserole to feed more people, you may want to use them.*

1	chicken (3 to 4 pounds) rinsed, patted dry, and cut into 6 pieces, wings and back reserved for another use (*see* figures 13 through 18, pages 58–60)
	Salt and ground black pepper
2	tablespoons extra-virgin olive oil
1	medium onion, chopped fine
3	medium garlic cloves, minced very fine
1½	cups long-grain white rice
1	can (14½ ounces) whole tomatoes, drained (about ½ cup liquid reserved) and chopped
½	cup white wine
⅓	cup chopped fresh parsley leaves

INSTRUCTIONS:

1. Preheat oven to 375 degrees. Sprinkle chicken pieces liberally on both sides with salt and pepper. Heat oil until shimmering in heavy, 12-inch skillet over high heat. Add chicken pieces skin side down; cook, without moving them, until well-browned, about 6 minutes. Turn chicken pieces over with tongs and cook, again without moving them, until well-browned on second side, about 6 minutes longer. Remove from pan and set aside.

2. Pour all but 2 tablespoons fat from pan; return to burner. Reduce heat to medium; add onion and sauté, stirring frequently, until softened, about 3 to 4 minutes. Add garlic and sauté until fragrant, approximately 1 minute longer. Stir in rice and cook, stirring frequently, until coated and glistening, about 1 minute longer.

3. Transfer rice mixture to 13 x 9-inch baking dish; add tomatoes. To skillet add reserved tomato liquid, wine, 1 teaspoon salt, and 2¼ cups water; increase heat to medium-high, scraping browned bits off pan bottom with wooden spoon. Bring to a boil and pour over rice mixture, stirring to combine.

4. Place chicken thighs and legs on top of the rice, cover tightly with foil, and bake for 20 minutes. Remove dish from oven, transfer chicken thighs and legs to plate, and stir rice (if rice appears too dry add ¼ cup more water and stir well). Add back chicken thighs and legs as well as breast pieces, re-cover, and cook until both rice and chicken pieces are tender, about 20 to 25 more minutes. Remove dish from oven. Stir in parsley, re-cover dish, and allow to rest for 5 minutes; serve immediately.

VARIATIONS:

Chicken and Rice Casserole with Saffron, Peas, and Paprika

Brown chicken as directed in Master Recipe. In step 2, along with onion, sauté 1 medium green bell pepper, cored, seeded, and cut into medium dice. Along with garlic, add 4 teaspoons paprika and ¼ teaspoon saffron and sauté until fragrant, about 1 minute. Proceed as directed, adding 1 cup thawed frozen peas along with parsley.

Chicken and Rice Casserole with Indian Spices

Brown chicken as directed in Master Recipe. At beginning of step 2, sauté one 3-inch piece cinnamon stick, stirring with wooden spoon until it unfurls, about 15 seconds. Add onion and 2 medium green bell peppers, stemmed, seeded, and cut into medium dice; sauté until onion and peppers are just soft, 5 to 6 minutes. Along with garlic, add 1 teaspoon each ground turmeric, coriander, and cumin. Proceed as directed, omitting parsley.

Chicken and Rice Casserole with Chiles, Cilantro, and Lime

Brown chicken as directed in Master Recipe. In step 2, along with onion, sauté 2 jalapeño chiles, cored, seeded, and minced. Along with garlic, add 2 teaspoons each ground cumin and coriander and 1 teaspoon chili powder and sauté until fragrant, about 1 minute. Proceed as directed, substituting ¼ cup chopped fresh cilantro leaves and 3 tablespoons lime juice for parsley.

Chicken and Rice Casserole with Anchovies, Olives, and Lemon

Brown chicken as directed in Master Recipe. In step 2, along with onions, sauté 5 minced anchovy fillets. Proceed as directed, adding 1 teaspoon minced lemon zest and 1 tablespoon juice from one small lemon and ½ cup imported black olives, pitted and halved, along with parsley.

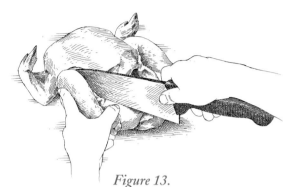

Figure 13.
We find that only breasts, thighs, and legs are worth using in a
casserole. We reserve the wings (along with the back) for making
stock. To butcher a chicken for a casserole, follow these steps.
With a sharp chef's knife, cut through the skin around the leg
where it attaches to the breast.

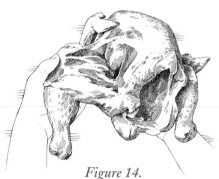

Figure 14.
Using your hand, pop each leg out of its socket.

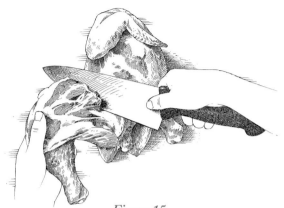

Figure 15.
Use your chef's knife to cut through the flesh and skin to detach each leg from the body.

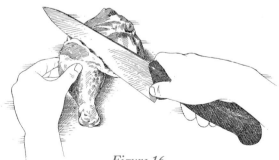

Figure 16.
A line of fat separates the thigh and drumstick. Cut through the joint at this point.

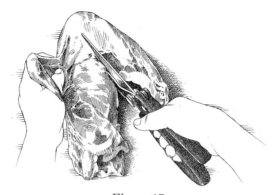

Figure 17.
Using poultry shears, cut down the ribs between the back and the breast to totally separate the back and wings from the breast. (Place back and wings in zipper-lock plastic bag and freeze to make stock when you have accumulated a few backs.)

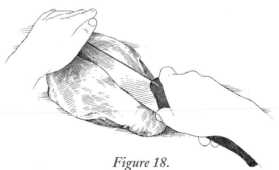

Figure 18.
Place a chef's knife directly on the breast bone, then apply pressure to cut through the bone and separate the breasts.

Jambalaya with Chorizo and Shrimp

serves 6

➤ NOTE: *This dish is delicious made with chorizo sausage, but andouille also works well. If you like hot foods, this recipe may not be spicy enough for you, so increase the cayenne as desired.*

1	tablespoon vegetable oil
8	ounces chorizo
1	large onion, finely diced
1	celery stalk, finely diced
1	medium red bell pepper, cored, seeded, and finely diced
3	medium garlic cloves, finely minced
1½	cups long-grain white rice
1	teaspoon salt
½	teaspoon minced fresh thyme leaves
½	teaspoon cayenne pepper
1	can (14½ ounces) whole tomatoes, drained and chopped
1	cup clam juice
1¾	cups chicken stock or low-sodium canned broth
1	large bay leaf
½	pound medium shrimp, shelled and (if desired) deveined
2	tablespoons minced fresh parsley leaves

:: INSTRUCTIONS:

1. Preheat oven to 375 degrees. Heat oil in heavy, 12-inch skillet over medium-high heat. Add chorizo; cook until sausage is fully rendered and nicely browned, approximately 7 to 8 minutes. Remove chorizo from pan and set aside to drain on a paper towel–lined plate.

2. Reduce heat to medium, add onion, celery, and red pepper, and cook until softened, 3 to 4 minutes. Add garlic and sauté until fragrant, about 1 minute longer. Stir in rice, salt, thyme, and cayenne, and cook, stirring frequently, until coated and glistening, about 1 minute longer. Transfer rice mixture to 13 x 9-inch baking dish; add tomatoes.

3. Add clam juice, chicken stock, bay leaf, and ½ cup water to skillet, increase heat to medium-high, scraping browned bits off pan bottom with wooden spoon. Bring to a boil and pour over rice mixture, adding chorizo and stirring to combine.

4. Cover tightly with foil and bake for 25 minutes. Remove dish from oven, stir the rice (if rice appears too dry add ¼ cup water and stir well), place shrimp on top of rice mixture, re-cover, and cook until rice is fully tender and shrimp is cooked, about 15 minutes more. Stir in parsley, re-cover dish, and allow to rest for 5 minutes. Remove bay leaf and serve immediately.

Barley and Mushroom Casserole with Sausage

serves 6

➤ NOTE: *This casserole is particularly starchy and filling.*

1	ounce dried porcini mushrooms
2	tablespoons extra-virgin olive oil
1	pound sweet Italian sausage, removed from casings
1	medium onion, chopped fine
3	medium garlic cloves, minced very fine
1	cup pearl barley
12	ounces white button mushrooms, sliced thin
½	cup white wine
1½	cups chicken stock or low-sodium canned broth
1	teaspoon salt
⅓	cup chopped fresh parsley leaves

░ INSTRUCTIONS:

1. Soak porcini mushrooms in 2 cups warm tap water in small bowl until softened, about 20 minutes. Lift mushrooms from liquid, chop mushrooms, and strain liquid, reserving 1 cup.

2. Preheat oven to 375 degrees. Heat oil until shimmering in heavy, 12-inch skillet over medium-high heat. Add sausage and cook, breaking it into ½-inch pieces, until well-browned all over, about 7 minutes. Remove from pan and set aside.

3. Lower heat to medium; add onion and sauté, stirring frequently, until softened, about 3 to 4 minutes. Add garlic and sauté until fragrant, approximately 1 minute longer. Stir in barley and cook, stirring frequently, until coated and glistening, about 1 minute longer.

4. Transfer barley mixture to 13 x 9-inch baking dish. Place empty skillet over medium-high heat, add button mushrooms, and cook, scraping browned bits off bottom of pan, until liquid evaporates, about 7 minutes. Add reserved porcini and their soaking liquid, wine, stock, and salt, bring to a boil, and pour over barley mixture.

5. Stir in sausage, cover tightly with foil, and bake for 20 minutes. Remove dish from oven, stir barley (if barley appears too dry, add ¼ cup water and mix well), re-cover, and bake until the barley is tender, about 20 to 25 minutes. Remove dish from oven. Stir in parsley, re-cover dish, and allow to rest for 5 minutes; serve immediately.

▓ VARIATION:

Barley and Mushroom Casserole with Chicken

Replace sausage with 1 chicken (3 to 4 pounds), rinsed, patted dry, and cut into 6 pieces, wings and backs reserved for another use (*see* figures 13 through 18, pages 58–60). Sprinkle chicken pieces liberally with salt and ground black pepper. Heat oil until shimmering in large, heavy skillet over high heat. Add chicken pieces skin side down; cook, without moving them, until well-browned, about 6 minutes. Turn chicken pieces over with tongs and cook, again without moving them, until well-browned on second side, about 6 minutes longer. Remove from pan and set aside. Pour all but 2 tablespoons fat from pan; return to burner and proceed with recipe, adding chicken thighs and legs to top of barley mixture for the first 20 minutes of cooking, then adding the chicken breast pieces for the next 20 to 25 minutes. Finish recipe as directed.

Sausage and Polenta Casserole
serves 6 to 8

➤ **NOTE:** *This casserole is very rich. It produces a "soft" polenta pie that does not slice well but should be spooned onto a plate. The polenta for the "crust" does not need to be fully cooked—it should remain soft enough to spread into a baking dish. Once the polenta is removed from the heat it will start to stiffen, so work quickly. If the polenta for the top "crust" stiffens too much as you make the bottom layer and spoon in the filling, stir in a small amount of hot water to achieve a more fluid consistency.*

Filling

2	tablespoons extra-virgin olive oil
1	medium garlic clove, minced
½	pound sweet Italian sausage, removed from casings
¼	cup minced fresh parsley leaves
	Salt
1	can (28 ounces) whole tomatoes packed in juice, drained (reserve juice) and chopped

Crust

2	tablespoons butter, plus extra for greasing baking dish
1	teaspoon salt
1	cup chicken stock or low-sodium canned broth

66

1½ cups yellow cornmeal
2 cups grated mozzarella cheese
¼ cup grated Parmesan cheese

▓ INSTRUCTIONS:

1. *For the filling:* Heat oil in a heavy, 12-inch skillet over medium heat; add the garlic and sauté until fragrant, about 1 minute. Add sausage, parsley, and ½ teaspoon salt; crumble sausage with edge of wooden spoon to break it apart into tiny pieces. Cook, continuing to crumble sausage, just until it loses its raw color but has not browned, about 3 minutes.

2. Add tomatoes and their juice and bring to a simmer; simmer until sauce begins to thicken, about 20 minutes. Adjust seasonings with extra salt to taste.

3. Preheat oven to 400 degrees. Butter 13 x 9-inch baking dish.

4. *For the crust:* Melt butter in large saucepan. Add 3 cups water and salt and bring to a boil. Mix chicken stock with 1 cup cold water in large measuring cup. Place cornmeal in medium bowl and slowly stir chicken stock mixture into cornmeal. Mix moistened cornmeal mixture into boiling water, stirring frequently over low heat until thickened, 15 to 18 minutes.

5. Assemble casserole according to figures 19–21. Bake until topping becomes golden brown and filling is bubbling, 30 to 40 minutes. Let casserole cool and solidify for 10 minutes before serving.

■ VARIATION:

Beef and Polenta Casserole
Follow Master Recipe, replacing sausage with ½ pound ground beef chuck.

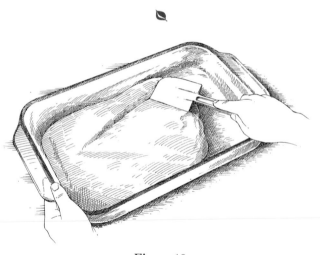

Figure 19.
Use a rubber spatula to spread half of the polenta mixture onto
the bottom of a buttered baking dish. The polenta crust should be
about ½ inch thick.

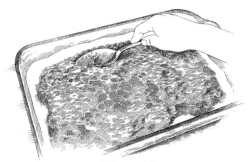

Figure 20.

*Carefully spoon the sausage filling over the polenta crust, leaving a
½-inch border around the edges. Gently press down on the filling
with the back of a spoon to push the polenta about ¼ inch up the
sides of the baking dish.*

Figure 21.

*Sprinkle half of the cheese over the filling. Spoon the remaining
polenta into the dish. Use a rubber spatula to spread the polenta
evenly over the filling to form a thin top crust. Make sure to push the
polenta to the edges of the dish so that it attaches to the raised portion
of the bottom crust. Sprinkle the remaining cheese over the polenta.*

chapter five

ろ

BEAN
CASSEROLES

BEANS MAKE A HEARTY BASE FOR CASSEROLES. Since casseroles are meant to be prepared relatively quickly, we wanted to figure out how to use canned or frozen beans in these recipes. We found that canned white and black beans are surprisingly good in casseroles. (Kidney beans also work well.) All of these beans remain fairly firm, even when baked. We tested several leading brands and found that Green Giant and Goya rated highest.

We had thought that organic beans made with far less sodium (many canned beans seem quite salty) would do well in this tasting. However, we found these beans to be bland and chalky. For the best flavor, salt should be added during the cooking process, whether beans are cooked at home or by a food manufacturer.

The other alternative to cooking dried beans is using frozen. We find that frozen lima beans and black-eyed peas are firmer and more flavorful than canned versions. Unlike white, black, and kidney beans, which are much sturdier, these two legumes don't seem to take well to canning.

Bean casseroles go hand in hand with pork. We used cooked ham for most of the recipes in this chapter, but we also tried smoked ham. While the smoked ham intensified the flavor of the casserole, it also added a saltiness that some tasters found objectionable. We prefer to stick with cooked ham.

This chapter includes recipes for three different kinds of bean casseroles. We find that beans alone are not satisfying as a casserole. They need help from another starch. We developed recipes that pair beans with toasted bread crumbs, rice, and cornbread to create one-dish meals.

The white bean casserole is the easiest to prepare. A quick bean stew (sautéed aromatics, drained canned beans, tomatoes, and stock) is spooned into a baking dish, sprinkled with bread crumbs, and baked.

Hoppin' John, a bean and rice casserole from South Carolina, is a bit more complex. The rice is handled as it is in the rice casserole recipes in the previous chapter. The black-eyed peas are stirred into the rice along with the liquid ingredients, and the mixture is baked in a casserole dish. This dish is appropriate year-round but is traditionally served on New Year's Day. The peas are supposed to bring good luck for the coming year.

The third type of casserole in this chapter combines a lima bean stew with a thick cornmeal batter that bakes into a cornbread topping. We tried cooking the lima beans in a roux base (flour and butter), but the flavor of the roux overwhelmed the lima beans. We found that the beans were better matched with chicken stock and a little cream.

The topping is a simple cornbread batter that should not be allowed to cover the filling completely. This is because the cream in the filling can cause it to become a bit watery. It's best if the batter is dropped by the spoonful over the filling (as if making a cobbler) so that some liquid from the sauce can evaporate in the oven. The result is a nicely thickened sauce that surrounds the beans and vegetables.

White Bean Casserole with Ham

serves 6

➤ **NOTE:** *Coarse homemade breadcrumbs make the best topping for this casserole; store-bought breadcrumbs are too fine and easily soak into the filling. Smoked ham lends nice flavor, but it is often very salty; if you use it, season the filling with care.*

Topping

2	cups coarse fresh bread crumbs (*see* figures 9 through 11, pages 38–39)
2	tablespoons unsalted butter, melted
½	cup grated Parmesan cheese

Filling

1	tablespoon butter, plus extra for greasing baking dish
1	tablespoon vegetable oil
2	medium onions, finely chopped
3	medium garlic cloves, minced very fine
12	ounces cooked ham, cut into ½-inch dice (about 2½ cups)
1	cup chicken stock or canned low-sodium broth
1	can (14.5 ounces) diced tomatoes, drained
3	cans (15 ounces each) white beans, drained and rinsed

1½   teaspoons minced fresh thyme
      Salt and ground black pepper

⁞⁞ INSTRUCTIONS:

1. *For the topping:* Adjust oven rack to upper-middle position and heat oven to 400 degrees. Mix bread crumbs and butter together in baking dish; bake until light golden brown and crisp, 5 to 8 minutes. Cool to room temperature, transfer to bowl, and mix with Parmesan cheese; set aside.

2. *For the filling:* Butter 13 x 9-inch baking dish and set it aside. Heat butter and oil in heavy, 12-inch skillet over medium-high heat until foam subsides; add onion and sauté until softened, 3 to 4 minutes. Add garlic and ham; sauté until garlic is fragrant, about 1 minute. Stir in stock, tomatoes, beans, and thyme; season with salt and pepper to taste and bring to a simmer.

3. Transfer mixture to baking dish and bake uncovered until bubbling around edges, about 10 minutes. Sprinkle bread crumb mixture on top and bake until bread crumbs are toasted and deep golden brown, about 8 minutes longer. Cool casserole 5 to 10 minutes before serving.

▪▪ VARIATION:

White Bean Casserole with Ham and Kale

Wash, stem, and shred 1 bunch kale (about 10 ounces) into ¼- to ½-inch strips. Follow Master Recipe, adding kale to skillet after onion has softened; sauté kale until wilted, 3 to 4 minutes. Add garlic and ham and proceed as directed.

Hoppin' John
serves 6

➤ NOTE: *Frozen black-eyed peas are used here because canned peas do not maintain their texture or shape in the oven.*

	Butter for greasing baking dish
1	tablespoon vegetable oil
6	ounces cooked ham, cut into ½-inch dice (about 1¼ cups)
3–4	slices bacon, diced
1	medium onion, chopped fine
3	medium garlic cloves, minced very fine
1½	cups long-grain white rice
½	teaspoon dried thyme
½	teaspoon hot red pepper flakes
2	bay leaves
2	cups chicken stock or low-sodium canned broth
1	teaspoon salt
	Ground black pepper
1	package (10 ounces) frozen black-eyed peas, thawed and rinsed
2	tablespoons minced fresh parsley leaves

⁑ INSTRUCTIONS:

1. Preheat oven to 375 degrees. Butter 13 x 9-inch baking dish and set it aside. Heat oil until shimmering in heavy, 12-inch skillet over medium-high heat. Add ham and cook until crisp and fat has rendered, about 6 minutes. Add bacon and cook until slightly crisp, about 3 minutes. Use slotted spoon to remove ham and bacon from pan and set aside on paper towel–lined plate.

2. Spoon out all but 2 tablespoons fat from pan; return to burner. Reduce heat to medium; add onion and sauté, stirring frequently, until softened, 3 to 4 minutes. Add garlic and sauté until fragrant, approximately 1 minute longer. Stir in rice, thyme, and red pepper flakes, and cook, stirring frequently until coated and glistening, about 1 minute longer. Transfer rice mixture to baking dish; add bay leaves.

3. Return skillet to heat; add chicken stock, 1½ cups water, salt, and pepper to taste. Increase heat to medium-high, scraping browned bits off bottom of pan with wooden spoon. Add black-eyed peas, ham, and bacon, bring to a boil, and pour over rice mixture, stirring to combine.

4. Cover tightly with foil and bake for 20 minutes. Remove from oven, stir the rice (if rice appears too dry add ¼ cup more water), re-cover with foil, and cook until the rice is fully tender, about 20 to 25 minutes more. Remove dish from oven. Stir in parsley, re-cover dish, and allow to rest for 5 to 10 minutes; serve immediately.

Sausage, Corn, and Lima Bean Casserole with Cornbread Crust

serves 6 to 8

➤ **NOTE:** *This casserole is quite rich and hearty. The filling is a creamy bean, corn, tomato, and sausage stew, while the topping is like moist cornbread.*

Filling

1	tablespoon vegetable oil
1	pound kielbasa sausage, halved lengthwise and cut into ¼-inch half moons
2	medium onions, finely chopped
4	medium garlic cloves, minced
2	teaspoons minced fresh thyme leaves
2	teaspoons minced fresh rosemary
1	cup chicken stock or low-sodium canned broth
½	cup heavy cream
1	can (14.5 ounces) whole tomatoes, drained and chopped
2	packages (10 ounces each) frozen lima beans, thawed and rinsed
1	package (10 ounces) frozen corn, thawed

Topping

½	cup yellow or white cornmeal
½	cup all-purpose flour
1	teaspoon baking powder
¼	teaspoon baking soda
2	teaspoons sugar
¼	teaspoon salt
1	large egg
⅓	cup buttermilk
⅓	cup milk
1	tablespoon unsalted butter, melted, plus extra for greasing baking dish

:: INSTRUCTIONS:

1. Preheat oven to 400 degrees. Butter 13 x 9-inch baking dish and set it aside.

2. *For the filling:* Heat oil until simmering in heavy, 12-inch skillet over medium-high heat. Add sausage and sauté, stirring occasionally with wooden spoon until sausage is evenly browned and fully rendered, 5 to 7 minutes. Remove sausage from pan and drain on paper towel–lined plate. Set aside.

3. Pour all but 2 tablespoons fat from pan; return to burner. Reduce heat to medium; add onions and cook until softened, 3 to 4 minutes. Add garlic, thyme, and rosemary and cook until fragrant, about 1 minute. Add chicken stock and cream, then increase heat to medium-high, scraping browned bits off pan bottom with wooden spoon. Stir in tomatoes, lima beans, and corn. Bring to a boil, then pour mixture into baking dish. Add sausage and stir to combine well. Cover with foil while preparing topping.

4. *For the topping:* Mix dry ingredients in medium bowl. Make a well in cornmeal mixture and add egg. Stir lightly with wooden spoon, then add buttermilk and milk. Stir wet and dry ingredients quickly until almost combined. Add melted butter; stir until ingredients are just combined.

5. Drop batter by large spoonfuls over lima bean filling, creating a cobblerlike topping (*see* figure 22). Bake until cornbread topping is golden brown, 20 to 25 minutes. Let rest for 5 to 10 minutes before serving.

Figure 22.
Drop the cornmeal batter by large spoonfuls over the filling.
Make sure to space the spoonfuls of batter evenly over the filling,
as if making a cobbler. The topping will spread in the oven,
covering most but not all of the filling.

chapter six

❧

POTATO CASSEROLES

HIS CHAPTER INCLUDES CASSEROLES IN which potatoes are the star. We begin with a recipe for shepherd's pie—basically, lamb stew topped with mashed potatoes. Traditional recipes for shepherd's pie start with leftover roast leg of lamb. We wanted to develop a recipe that did not start with leftovers that many cooks are unlikely to have. We tested ground lamb, and although this made a credible filling, it was not as richly flavored and toothsome as we wanted. We then tested meaty (and relatively inexpensive) shoulder chops, which are our favorite for lamb stew. They worked beautifully, giving the filling a hearty lamb flavor and chewy (but not tough texture) that contrasts nicely with the smooth mashed potato topping.

We tried using regular mashed potatoes as the topping for this casserole, but they started to break down in the oven. Adding two egg yolks gives the mashed potatoes more body and helps them hold their shape.

Scalloped potatoes, thinly sliced rounds of potatoes baked with dairy and usually cheese, are a classic side dish. To bring this dish up to the level of a main course, we devised two different strategies. Our first was to layer many more potatoes than is customary into the casserole dish. This worked just fine. Our second concerned the "sauce" for the potatoes, which is traditionally made from heavy cream. We found that this worked fine, although we felt the rich cream needed some contrasting flavors. Simmering a little garlic, cayenne, nutmeg, salt, and pepper in the cream added the extra level of flavor we thought was needed.

To make sure that all of the potatoes in this recipe (almost five pounds) fit into the baking dish, it is necessary to layer the slices with some care. We also found it helpful to compress the layers with a spatula several times during baking. This gives the casserole a substantial texture, while also allowing the cream to circulate completely around the potatoes, helping to brown the top layer.

The New England Scalloped Fish and Potato Casserole is less fussy than the all-potato scallop because there is no layering of the potatoes in the pan. The potatoes need to be parcooked on the stove top so that the fish does not over-cook. At this point, the potatoes slices are simply poured into the baking dish, the fish is added, and the casserole is briefly baked. This dish is also looser than the potato scallop because the sauce does not cook down so much in the oven.

As for flavoring these scalloped potato casseroles, we prefer bacon. Ham could be used, but we like the strong, salty flavor of bacon best. We found that the fish casserole also benefited from the addition of smoked trout, which added another level of seafood flavor to this dish.

Shepherd's Pie

serves 6 to 8

➤ NOTE: *We found that diced lamb shoulder chops give the fill-ing a much richer flavor than ground lamb. If you prefer to use ground lamb, see the variation on page 87. Follow the assembly instructions below, or, for a fancier presentation, see figures 24 through 26, pages 88–89.*

Filling

3	pounds lamb shoulder chops (4 chops), boned and cut into 1-inch pieces (should yield about 1½ pounds)
1½	teaspoons salt
1	teaspoon ground black pepper
3	tablespoons vegetable oil
2	medium onions, chopped coarse
2	medium carrots, cut into ¼-inch slices
1	garlic clove, finely minced
2	tablespoons all-purpose flour
1	tablespoon tomato paste
2¼	cups chicken stock or low-sodium canned broth
¼	cup full-bodied red wine
1	teaspoon Worcestershire sauce
1	teaspoon fresh chopped thyme
1	teaspoon fresh chopped rosemary
1	cup frozen peas, thawed

Topping

2	pounds large russet potatoes, peeled and cut into 2-inch cubes
1	teaspoon salt
6	tablespoons unsalted butter, softened
¾	cup whole milk, warmed
2	large egg yolks
	Ground black pepper

INSTRUCTIONS:

1. Season lamb with salt and pepper. Heat 2 tablespoons oil until shimmering in 12-inch skillet over medium-high heat. Add half of lamb and cook, until well-browned on all sides, 5 to 6 minutes. Remove from pan and set aside. Put remaining tablespoon oil into pan and cook remaining lamb, again until well-browned on all sides, 5 to 6 minutes. Remove from pan and set aside with previously cooked lamb.

2. Reduce heat to medium and add onion and carrot to fat in now-empty pan. Cook until softened, about 4 minutes. Add garlic, flour, and tomato paste, and cook until garlic is fragrant and flour is cooked, about 1 minute. Whisk in stock and wine, then Worcestershire sauce. Stir in thyme, rosemary, and reserved lamb. Bring to a boil, cover tightly with lid, then reduce heat to low and simmer until lamb is just tender, 25 to 30 minutes.

3. Meanwhile, put potatoes in large saucepan; add cold water to cover and ½ teaspoon salt. Bring to a boil and continue to cook over medium heat until potatoes are tender when pierced with knife, 15 to 20 minutes. Drain potatoes well and return pan to low heat. Mash potatoes over low heat, adding butter as you mash. Stir in warm milk and then egg yolks. Season with ½ teaspoon salt and ground pepper to taste.

4. Preheat oven to 400 degrees. Stir peas into lamb mixture and check seasonings. Pour evenly into 13 x 9-inch baking dish. With a large spoon, place mashed potatoes over entire filling. Starting at sides to make sure of a tight seal, use rubber spatula to smooth out potatoes (*see* figure 23, page 88). Bake until top turns golden brown, 20 to 25 minutes. Let pie rest 5 to 10 minutes before serving.

▓ VARIATION:
Shepherd's Pie with Ground Lamb
Follow Master Recipe, substituting 1½ pounds ground lamb for the lamb shoulder chops. Cook, one half at a time, until well-browned, about 3 minutes for each batch of lamb. Continue with recipe as directed, reducing simmering time in step 2 to 15 minutes.

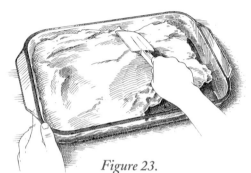

Figure 23.

Spoon the mashed potatoes over the entire filling. Starting at the sides of the baking dish, use a rubber spatula to spread the potatoes into an even layer. Make sure that the potatoes attach to the sides of the dish and that you can't see the filling.

Figure 24.

For a fancier presentation, we like to bake shepherd's pie in a 10-inch pie plate. The mashed potato topping rises high above the filling, much like a lemon meringue pie or baked Alaska. Place the filling in the pie plate and then drop spoonfuls of mashed potatoes around the perimeter of the pie plate.

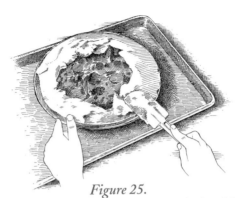

Figure 25.
Use a rubber spatula to attach the potatoes to the rim of the pie plate. It's important to seal the edges this way to prevent the filling from bubbling out of the pie plate in the oven.

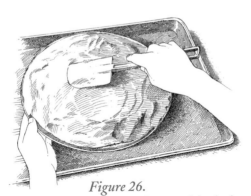

Figure 26.
Drop the remaining mashed potatoes in the center of the pie plate and then smooth the top with a spatula. Because the topping rises so high, we recommend baking the pie on a baking sheet to catch any drips.

Hearty Scalloped Potatoes
serves 6 to 8

➤ **NOTE:** *The larger chunks of bread (as opposed to bread crumbs) work well with the scalloped potatoes. We prefer smoky bacon in this dish, although you could use diced cooked ham instead. To use ham, sauté the onions and garlic in a tablespoon of vegetable oil and then add 1½ cups diced ham and heat it through.*

Topping

3	slices white bread (3 ounces), crusts removed and cut into ¼-inch dice
3	tablespoons unsalted butter, melted
1	cup grated Parmesan cheese

Filling

6	ounces bacon, diced
2	small onions, minced
2	medium garlic cloves, minced
3	cups heavy cream
1½	teaspoons salt
½	teaspoon ground black pepper
	Pinch cayenne pepper
¼	teaspoon nutmeg
4½–5	pounds medium-large russet potatoes, peeled and cut into ¼-inch slices
3 ½	ounces Gruyère cheese, shredded

⚏ INSTRUCTIONS:

1. *For the topping:* Adjust oven rack to middle position and heat oven to 350 degrees. Mix bread cubes and melted butter in small baking dish; bake until golden brown and crisp, about 20 minutes. Cool to room temperature, transfer to bowl, and mix with Parmesan. Keep oven on.

2. *For the filling:* Cook bacon in medium skillet over medium heat until crisp and fat has fully rendered, 5 to 6 minutes. Transfer bacon to paper towel–lined plate. Pour off all but 1 tablespoon fat from pan. Add onions and sauté until golden brown, 3 to 4 minutes. Add half of garlic and sauté until fragrant, about 1 minute. Set aside.

3. In medium saucepan, heat cream, remaining garlic, 1¼ teaspoons salt, black pepper, cayenne pepper, and nutmeg until simmering. Remove from heat.

4. Arrange half of potatoes in bottom of 13 x 9-inch baking dish, forming 3 to 4 long rows of densely overlapping slices (*see* figure 27, page 92). Sprinkle slices with ¼ teaspoon salt and black pepper to taste. Sprinkle potato layer evenly with the sautéed onions, bacon, and Gruyère. With remaining potatoes, arrange a second layer over filling, creating a snug cover of overlapping rows reaching edges of baking dish (*see* figure 28, page 93). Pour hot cream mixture over potatoes.

5. Bake until cream thickens and top turns deep golden brown, about 1 hour and 15 minutes, pressing surface of casserole twice with spatula to make cream on bottom of dish rise to surface (*see* figure 29). Sprinkle top with crouton mixture and bake for 5 minutes. Let rest for 5 to 10 minutes before serving.

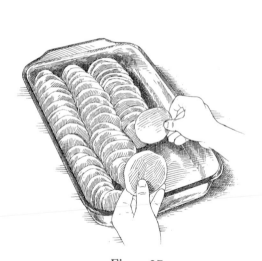

Figure 27.
Arrange half of potatoes in bottom of baking dish, forming 3 to 4 long rows of densely overlapping slices. Make sure that potato slices go right to the sides of the dish to form a tight crust.

Figure 28.

Sprinkle filling over bottom layer of potatoes. Add a second layer of overlapping potato slices, making sure that crust extends right to the edges of the dish.

Figure 29.

As the potato casserole bakes, occasionally press down on the top of the casserole with a spatula to force the cream on the bottom of the baking dish up. This technique will keep the top layer of potatoes moist and will also bind the layers together to form a slightly compressed cake that holds together when sliced.

93

New England Scalloped Fish and Potato Casserole

serves 6 to 8

➤ NOTE: *Cod is traditional here, but haddock or any other firm, flaky white fish could be substituted. The smoked trout in the recipe adds a cured, sweet flavor, almost like ham, that works especially well with cod.*

Topping

3	slices white bread (3 ounces), crusts removed and cut into ¼ inch dice
3	tablespoons unsalted butter, melted

Filling

4	ounces bacon, diced
2	small onions, minced
2	medium celery stalks, minced
1	garlic clove, minced
3	tablespoons all-purpose flour
1½	cups chicken stock or low-sodium canned broth
1	cup heavy cream
¼	cup white wine
1	bay leaf
1½	pounds medium-large russet potatoes, peeled and cut into ¼-inch slices
1½	pounds cod fillets, cut into 1-inch cubes

4   ounces smoked trout, flaked
Salt and ground black pepper

⁂ INSTRUCTIONS:

1. *For the topping:* Adjust oven rack to middle position and heat oven to 350 degrees. Mix bread cubes and melted butter in small baking dish; bake until golden brown and crisp, about 20 minutes. Cool to room temperature and set aside.

2. *For the filling:* Cook bacon in Dutch oven over medium heat until crisp and fat has fully rendered, 5 to 6 minutes. Use slotted spoon to transfer to paper towel lined–plate. Still over medium heat, add onions and celery and cook until softened, 4 to 5 minutes. Add garlic and cook until fragrant, about 1 minute. Stir in flour and cook until golden, about 1 minute.

3. Whisk in stock, cream, and wine. Add bay leaf, reserved bacon, and potatoes. Bring to a boil, then reduce heat to medium-low. Cover and cook until potatoes are just tender, about 15 minutes. Remove and discard bay leaf.

4. Stir in cod, trout, and salt and pepper to taste. Pour into 13 x 9- inch baking dish. Cover tightly with foil; bake until cream thickens and cod is fully cooked, 15 to 20 minutes. Uncover dish. Sprinkle top with croutons and bake, uncovered, for 5 minutes. Let rest 5 to 10 minutes before serving.

index